THE NIGHT FOUNTAIN

Salvatore Quasimodo

THE NIGHT FOUNTAIN

LA FONTANA NOTTURNA

SELECTED EARLY POEMS

Introduced and translated by
Marco Sonzogni and Gerald Dawe

Foreword by Alessandro Quasimodo

2008

Published by Arc Publications,
Nanholme Mill, Shaw Wood Road
Todmorden OL14 6DA, UK

Design by Tony Ward
Printed by Berforts Information Press, Ltd.

978 1904614 05 0 pbk
978 1904614 87 6 hbk

Cover illustration:
The Night Fountain (2007) by Julia Maria Seemann,
acrylic on canvas and collage, 12.5 x 17.5 cm

The publishers acknowledge financial assistance from
ACE Yorkshire.

Arc Publications' series
Arcania: New Translations of Classic Poets
Editors: Jean Boase-Beier & Philip Wilson

ACKNOWLEDGEMENTS

The Night Fountain is a selection of poems from the section 'Poesie disperse, inedite o non ripubblicate dall'autore' in: Salvatore Quasimodo. *Tutte le poesie*, edited by Gilberto Finzi (Milan: Mondadori, 1995, pp. 391-585). The Italian originals are reprinted here by kind permission of Alessandro Quasimodo and Mondadori. The following poems were published before their inclusion in the collected poems: 'L'aurora' (Dawn), 1915, published in *Humanitas*, Bari, 31 May 1917; 'Primule' (Wild flowers), in *Nuovo Giornale Letterario*, no. 3, June 1917; 'Sfioritura' (Withering), in *Nuovo Giornale Letterario*, no. 4, July 1917; 'Il colore del desiderio' (The colour of desire), c.1917, in *Il Marchesino*, Messina, 8 April 1922; 'Nascere' (Birth), in *Gazzetta del Popolo*, 17 August 1932; 'Candida foce' (Innocent mouth), 1931, in *Mirages*, Tunisi, II, nos. 3-4, Janurary-February 1934, together with its French translation 'Gorge candide' by Armand Guibert (this poem was also reprinted as an unpublished poem in *La Situazione*, Udine, no. 5, September 1958); 'Il fiore del silenzio' (The flower of silence), in *Il Marchesino*, Messina, 8 April 1922; 'Profanazione' (Profanation) in *Libere Idee*, November 1917; 'La porta chiusa' (The locked door) in *L'Albatro*, Messina, 24 June 1922.

Earlier versions of some of the translations in this volume appeared in the following journals: *College Green, Modern Poetry in Translation, Poetry Ireland Review, The Attic, The Stinging Fly* and *Translation Ireland*.

The translators would like to thank Jean Boase-Beier, Geoff Brock, Bob Lowe, Jamie McKendrick and Cormac Ó Cuilleanáin.

The publishers wish to thank the School of English and the Department of Italian, School of Languages, Literatures and Cultural Studies, University of Dublin, Trinity College, for funding to support the translation of this volume.

for Concetto

CONTENTS

Foreword / 11
Introduction / 14

FOREWORD
Alessandro Quasimodo

During a long stay in Messina in the summer of 1970 I thought I would trace the early cultural development of my father, Salvatore Quasimodo, by seeking out documents in the city where he went to school. It was in Messina, at the Istituto Tecnico "Jaci" that my father had a significant encounter with a sensitive and modern teacher of Italian, Frederico Rampollo del Tindaro who inspired the young Totò [Salvatore] to read beyond the school syllabus – readings that would open up for him a new world of images and words.

I looked without success in the library of Messina University; equally without success I visited one of my father's closest friends, Salvatore Pugliatti, the distinguished man of letters and law, who had custody of Quasimodo's early manuscripts as well as the originals of *I notturni del re silenzioso*.

Finally I succeeded thanks to a chance contact with Luigi Occhipinti who had owned a newsagent's store in Messina during the First World War; this store had stocked *Il nuovo giornale letterario*, a periodical founded by Quasimodo and his young friends and to which he had contributed with much enthusiasm.

More significantly, Occhipinti (in 1970 in his nineties) was the uncle of Giorgio La Pira, one of my father's school friends and someone who had significantly influenced my father's spiritual and moral growth. Totò had given La Pira a manuscript and then had forgotten all about it. The manuscript was of thirty-seven poems written between 1917 and 1920 and entitled *Bacia la soglia della sua casa*. When La Pira left Messina, the manuscript remained in his uncle's house.

Around Christmas 1970, Luigi Occhipinti (with fatherly affection and with his family's approval) gave me those unpublished poems and what had survived of the correspondence between my father and La Pira between 1920 and 1925. Before me was an object with a poetry of its own – frayed and faded sheets of paper, so orderly, even with page numbers in the table of contents and sealed with the young poet's signature – an artefact meticulously prepared by Quasimodo himself in his first entry into what was to be a lifetime profession. These poems were labelled 'pre-idyllic' by Elio Filippo

11

Accocca in his introduction to them. They contain the themes of escape and wandering, several autobiographical references ("sudden goodbyes" testifying to his changes of residence during those early years in Sicily) and hints of the poetic spirituality that was soon to emerge. Strongly represented as well are images of Arcadia, landscapes brimming with memories and vibrating with emotions, sounds that are intense and unmistakeable.

This poetry, both descriptive and narrative, is not yet mature. The young poet is still striving to attain the 'pure language' that both creates and evokes, speaking out loudly and independently in the void, and painting without delineating rigid contours.

Quasimodo's poetic pre-history, as it were, has remained locked in a drawer for a long time. Now, however, re-discovered and re-read, these poems testify to a precocious interest in poetry and a crossing of the *soglia della casa* – the domestic threshold – towards the infinity of language.

Salvatore Quasimodo at 18 (in 1919)

INDICE

Fine

Salvatore Quasimodo

13

LA PREGHIERA

Diventa buono, se vuoi ascoltare la mia voce,
e bacia la soglia della tua casa.

Porta due lampade, calde come il petto delle rondini,
e, verso sera, quando il tuo viso avrà la penombra del cielo,

apri il cancello di vetro del mio rifugio azzurro,
e, in silenzio, accostati a me.

Ti dirò dei miei sogni lasciati sopra gli scalini,
dietro le porte chiuse e sconosciute,
dei sogni sbocciati in poveri giardini,
senza canti, in mezzo a le cicute.

Poi, taci e ritorna: la musica che dorme sotto le mimose
si sveglierà per te, che hai baciato la soglia della tua casa

I

14

LA FONTANA NOTTURNA

Profumo di zagara chiusa, fontana notturna d'incanti,
io ti chiamo coi nomi dei fiori più fragili,
quando il sonno mi manca,
il mio pane con la croce bianca,
tutta di stelle e neve –

Quando, vispa, sui muri degli orti,
saltella
la lupinella,
io cerco tra il roseo i tuoi occhi
così calmi che sembrano d'una pecorella;

ma che mi fanno tanto male:
come le parole d'addio,
come le parole non dette
che restano nel cuore
per tema di trovarle poco affettuose.

Lasciai due baci sul tuo corpo d'orchidea,
che a me parvero due margheritine,
di quelle che stanno sui lembi delle strade
e sono piccole piccole ed hanno tanto freddo,
e fuori, il cielo a macchie scure e bianche come una pernice
aveva la mia febbre, e io credevo d'essere felice.

XXXVIII

Index and text of two early poems in the handwriting of the poet.

INTRODUCTION

I
FROM LIBRARY TO LIBRARY:
READING AND TRANSLATING QUASIMODO
Marco Sonzogni

One day in 2001, working in the library of Dublin's Istituto Italiano di Cultura, I came across a beautiful book: Salvatore Quasimodo, *Poems*. The slim, pamphlet-like volume – whose brown cover had been yellowed by almost forty years of shelf-life – contained a selection of Quasimodo's poetry translated into Irish and English. This elegant trilingual edition was published to mark the Nobel Laureate's visit to Ireland in February 1963. A few days later, this time in the library of Trinity College Dublin, I came across another special book: Salvatore Quasimodo, *Scritti sul teatro*. It was signed by the Sicilian poet on 28 February 1963, when he donated it to the University of Dublin's Italian Department on the occasion of his visit.

Quasimodo's presence and legacy in Ireland acted as a call to re-read his poetry some twenty-five years after first reading and studying it in school. And this call soon yielded to another, more compelling one: the call of translation.

The first step was to choose poems that had not been translated before. The existing Quasimodo in English – the remarkable efforts of Thomas G. Bergin, Jack Bevan, Edith Farnsworth, Charles Guenter, Allen Mandelbaum, Sandro Pacifici and others – limited the options. The section of *poesie disperse* (dispersed poems) included in Quasimodo's *Collected Poems*, therefore, was the obvious alternative and turned out to be more substantial than expected, both in terms of quality and quantity.

The second step was to call on an Irish poet to translate this new selection of Quasimodo's uncollected early poems. Gerald Dawe was one of the first contemporary writers I had been reading since I arrived in Ireland in 1993 as a visiting student in the School of English at Trinity College Dublin (where Dawe was, and is, a lecturer). His poetry struck me for his exact and sophisticated diction, and for the reassuring maturity with which he voices thoughts and feelings. And these, I felt, were the appropriate qualities to make sure that the expressive impulse and verbal exuberance of the young Quasimodo would be addressed and accounted for in earnest.

Gerald Dawe promptly answered the call of translation, responding to my mediation and, above all, to the enchanting energy of Quasimodo's original poems with the sensitivity and skills that make Dawe's own poetry so distinctive and enjoyable.

It is thanks to Dawe's gifts as a poet that these translations, too, have become distinctive and enjoyable poems.

II
FROM BOOKSHOP TO WORKSHOP:
READING AND TRANSLATING QUASIMODO
Gerald Dawe

There is a large bank building at the corner of Howard Street and Donegal Square in Belfast where the bookshop used to be. The book shop was called Gardiners, if memory serves me right, and most Saturday afternoons, and after school waiting for the 64 bus home, I called in there in the mid-Sixties to look at the new Penguins which had arrived. The black bulky Penguin Classics, the orangey-red novels, the somewhat austere Peregrines and the strangely frail looking play-texts. Also a series called Penguin Modern European Poets with their clear surname titles: RILKE *Selected Poems*, APOLLINAIRE, YEVTUSHENKO and QUASIMODO, all translated with valuable uncomplicated introductions.

It was a godsend. Reading these collections opened wide, very wide, the view for a young Belfast boy. And there was something in Quasimodo's verse, translated by Jack Bevan, that intrigued me even then. It was a language stripped of flamboyance and high-flown rhetoric, that was tacit and interior. "The signal achievement of Quasimodo," Jack Bevan remarked, "seems to be not so much his renewal of language as a development of a new attitude to it, a wiser reticence. He is concerned with speech, not song; organisation, not symmetry."

I'm not sure that would have meant so much to the teenager I was when I first read it. However, working on these early uncollected poems of Quasimodo's, and even allowing for their highly charged lyricism, I can see precisely what Jack Bevan meant. In Quasimodo's verse the landscape and sound of his own voice merge into, at times, a dreamy, mesmerical world, or, in the better known later poems, he speaks out with a succinct, concentrated fire. Either way, the control of the lyrical impulse is there to keep the poem in line, depth-charged, waiting to explode with passion or remorse or rage.

My contribution to the versions which follows was completely dependent upon Marco Sonzogni's diligent texts. I thank him for his invitation to collaborate with his work. I hardly thought over thirty years ago that I would have had such an opportunity to get so close to Salvatore Quasimodo's inner life as a poet. His poems have all the intimacy and strangeness of dreams and working on their translation into English made me realise how much is relinquished by sticking only to the everyday realities. The scents, colours and rituals of Quasimodo's verse really are forms of delight.

REFERENCES

S. Quasimodo. *Scritti sul teatro*. Milan: Mondadori, 1961.

The selected writings of Salvatore Quasimodo. Edited and translated from the Italian by A. Mandelbaum. New York: Farrar, Straus and Cudahy, 1960.

Thirty poems by Salvatore Quasimodo. Translated, and with an introduction, by C. Guenter, in *The Literary Review*, no. 3, Spring 1960, pp. 366-382.

S. Quasimodo. *Poems*. Translations into Irish by Ethna Byrne Costigan and Máirín and Cearbhall O'Dálaigh. Translations into English by G. H. McWilliam, Jennifer McWilliam, Ulick O'Connor and Lorna Reynolds. Contributions by Francesco Flora and by Anders Österling. Dublin: Istituto Italiano di Cultura, 1963.

S. Quasimodo. *The poet and the politician, and other essays*. Translated by T. G. Bergin and S. Pacifici. Carbondale: Southern Illinois University Press, 1964. S. Quasimodo. *Selected poems*. Translated and with an introduction by J. Bevan. Harmondsworth: Penguin, 1965 (Penguin Modern European Poets).

S. Quasimodo. *To give and to have, and other poems*. Translated by E. Farnsworth. Chicago: Regnery, 1969.

S. Quasimodo. *Debit and credit*. Translated and with an introduction by J. Bevan. London: Anvil Press Poetry in association with Routledge and Paul Kegan, 1972.

S. Quasimodo. *Complete poems*. Translated by J. Bevan. London: Anvil, 1983 and New York: Schocken, 1984.

THE NIGHT FOUNTAIN
LA FONTANA NOTTURNA

"The night is long that never finds the day."
Shakespeare, MACBETH

L'AURORA

Bianca, fugace, la nebbia svapora
nell'aria pura. S'indora l'oriente,
s'effonde la luce: ecco l'aurora.
L'ultimo grido il gufo alla fuggente
tenebra getta e nel silente ombroso
bosco dispare. Incomincia l'amore
allegri trillano fra l'odoroso
aere dei giovani arbusti in fiore
gli uccelli. Si drizzan sullo stelo
superbi i sonnecchianti ciclamini,
aspettando impazienti che nel cielo
turchino, luminoso l'astro d'oro
sorga a schiudere i loro corallini
petali. È la rosea aurora: al lavoro!

DAWN

White fleeting fog evaporates
in the clear air. The east turns golden
and the light spreads: it's dawn.
The owl lets out the last scream
to the fugitive dark and disappears
in the silent shady wood. Love begins
and birds sing happily in the scented air
of the young blossomed shrubs.
The dozing cyclamens stand proud
on their stems and impatiently wait
for the shining golden star
to rise in the deep blue sky
to open their coral petals.
It's the crimson dawn: to work!

PRIMULE

Grumi pensili di sangue sul lacero velluto verdognolo.
Oh le ferite dei prati!
La primavera respirando voluttuosamente l'aria soave, ha rotte
le vene del suo seno turgido.
Un fiotto di vento con le labbra avide; un bacio! E le
primule sanguigne galleggiano su l'onde filamentose e
senza spuma.

WILD FLOWERS

Blood clots hanging over torn green velvet:
the wounds of the fields!
Breathing in the sweet air, spring has broken
the veins of its swollen breasts.
Wind gusts with eager lips: a kiss!
Blood-red wild flowers float on threadlike
and foamless waves.

SFIORITURA

Oh l'orchidea cristallina
del mio sogno,
sbocciata nel vespero
agonizzante
intriso di sangue,
striato
da fili di latte
coagulato;
sfiorita ne la sera
fuligginosa, senza trilli metallici
d'usignoli,
senza voli
di capinera,
senza tremuli tintinni
di sonagli opalini
della veste celeste
abbrunata d'una dama misteriosa!...

Oh l'orchidea!
In un'alba imbellettata
di biacca rosata
con le labbra violacee
da brividi alitanti di gelo,
rividi i petali biancastri, malaticci
del mio sogno iridescente
imputriditi laggiù
nel palude affogato
di limo – calice
di lacrime salmastre stillate
da un salice
che non piange più!

WITHERING

The crystal orchid
of my dream,
blossomed in the dying
evening,
blood-soaked,
streaked
with threads of sour
milk;
withered in the smokey
evening, without the metallic trill
of the nightingales,
without the flights
of the blackcaps,
without the trembling
of opal bells
in the sky-blue, dark
bodice of a mysterious lady!…

The orchid!
At a dawn painted
with rosy powder,
my lips made violet
by shivering breaths of cold,
I saw again the white petals, sick
with my iridescent dreams
rotten down there
in the marsh drowned
with lime – chalice
of salty tears dripping
from a willow
that no longer cries!

IL COLORE DEL DESIDERIO

S'accese, ne la notte, una canzone:
come una stella; ero io triste
e tu piangevi, donna d'altra terra.

Non bastava il mio amore al tuo deserto;
no, come dicevi quand'eri presso al sonno,
umile come sandalo d'asceta.

Amavi il mare, nomade scontenta,
che le vele, a sera, facevano giardino
di freschissimi gigli,
amavi il vento che, come boccuccia di pargolo
(maternità, dolore che dà luce!)
di marmo roseo scolpiva i tuoi capezzoli,
germoglio di tutti gli aromi,
mia piccola foresta di fontane.

Io pure conosco il tuo dolore:
cammino, e più luce mi pare che sia
nel cielo lasciato per altro
che più vivo di sole, sembrava.

THE COLOUR OF DESIRE

A song lit up in the night,
like a star; I was sad and you
were crying, lady from another country.

My love wasn't enough for your desert;
it wasn't, as you said when you were falling asleep,
humble like the sandal of a hermit.

You loved the sea, unhappy nomad,
that, in the evening, sails turned into a garden
of freshest lilies;
you loved the wind that, like the little mouth of a child
(motherhood, sorrow that gives light!),
sculpted the pink marble of your nipples,
blossom of all scents,
my little forest of fountains.

I too know your sorrow:
I walk and seem to see more light
in the sky left however
more lively with the sun, or so it seemed.

NASCERE

Naufragio d'alberi rosei,
muover della luce,
inizio dolce di giorno,
all'erbe, all'acque dono
di letizia.

Gonfia il cielo in nuvole e foglie;
urlano buie le macchine
piene di nebbia:
pena più grande
non porta il mio cuore.

Lieve fermento mi ascolto:
a specchio del verde
dirama di vene e di fiori
una rete;

amorosa respira:
la voce
è il primo tremare dell'aria.

BIRTH

Shipwreck of rosy trees,
mover of light,
sweet start of the day,
for the grass, for the water
a gift of joy.

The sky swells with clouds and leaves;
dark cars full of fog groan:
my heart couldn't bear
a heavier pain.

A light ferment, I listen to myself:
a mirror to the green
a net of veins and flowers
that branches out;

yearning, breathing:
the voice
is the first shiver in the air.

CANDIDA FOCE

Candida foce
su cui posa in gioco
una mano non mia, dimenticata.

Male anche la neve;
silenzio più stanco
il crollo di foglie mature.

Tardi nel cuore, e ogni cosa
forma che duole immobile,
e un altro volto vita da lasciare.

Un vento bianca questa morte
sollevi,
la terra il suono di fontane.

INNOCENT MOUTH

Innocent mouth
on which a hand not mine rests,
in play, forgotten.

The snow too is bad;
a wearier silence
the fall of spent leaves.

Late in the heart, and everything
is a form that hurts, immobile,
and another face a life to leave.

Let the wind raise
this white death,
the earth the sound of fountains.

LA PREGHIERA

Diventa buono, se vuoi ascoltare la mia voce,
e bacia la soglia della tua casa.

Porta due lampade, calde come il petto delle rondini,
e, verso sera, quando il tuo viso avrà la penombra del cielo

apri il cancello di vetro del mio rifugio azzurro,
e, in silenzio, accostati a me.

Ti dirò dei miei sogni lasciati sopra gli scalini,
dietro le porte chiuse e sconosciute,
dei sogni sbocciati in poveri giardini,
senza canti, in mezzo a le cicute.

Poi, taci e ritorna: la musica che dorme sotto le mimose
si sveglierà per te, che hai baciato la soglia della tua casa.

PRAYER

Be good now if you want to hear my voice,
and kiss the doorstep of your home.

Bring two lamps, warm like the breast of the swallow,
and, when evening comes, when your face has the shade of the sky,

open the glass gate of my blue refuge
and, silent, come near.

I will tell you of the dreams I left on the steps,
behind closed and unknown doors,
of the dreams that blossomed in poor gardens,
without songs, among hemlocks.

Then be silent and go back: the music sleeping under the mimosa
will awake for you, who have kissed the doorstep of your home.

L'OFFERTA DIVINA

La notte, nelle pallide mani di nomade,
mi porse un ramoscello fiorito di stelle.

L'impronta dei passi
ch'era morta su le strade del sogno,
come i templi sepolti,
si risvegliò, bianca di rugiada, su la terra.

E l'occhio, aperto tristemente
nei silenzi che non erano mai perfetti,
si chiuse e si riposò al profumo
che venne certo lontano da noi.

Tu femina, che non sei l'oblìo
e pure dai una piccola stella d'azzurro,
accanto all'offerta divina
diventi cenere, come l'acqua del lago
quando vi si specchia dentro la sera
senza incantesimo di gemme.

DIVINE OFFER

The night passed into my pale nomadic hands
a twig flowered with stars.

The footprint
that died on the roads of dream,
like buried temples,
awoke again, white with dew, on the earth.

And the eye, opened sadly
in silences that were never perfect,
closed and rested in the scent
that came so far away from us.

You, lass, who aren't oblivion
and yet give a small star of blue,
beside the divine offer
become ashes, like lake water
when the evening is a mirror
without the enchantment of precious stones.

IL SILENZIO DEGLI SCHIAVI

Notte, o calice azzurro di musica,
fiori portiamo ai tuoi altari di cenere,
or che le lampade d'oro
a le porte dei tempî sono accese.

Con diverse cadenze,
diciamo ciò che, in natura, è la stessa cosa;
ma sul cammino, la luce era del sole,
l'acqua che addormentò la nostra sete
era fiore di roccia sempre fresco,
e l'acqua, come il sole, era la stessa.

Dacci silenzio pei nostri divini convegni;
lo schiavo che, nella casa lontana,
lasciò l'ultimo sogno come un fuoco acceso,
sa anche pregare, sorella buona
che chiudi gli occhi ai fanciulli
ne l'ora che chiudi le rose.

THE SILENCE OF SLAVES

Night, blue chalice of music,
we bring flowers to your altars of ashes,
now that the golden lamps
at the doors of the temples are lit.

With different rhythms,
we say what in nature is the same thing;
but along the way, the light belonged to the sun,
the water that quenched our thirst
was an ever-fresh flower of the rock,
and the water, like the sun, was the same.

Give us silence for our divine meetings;
the slave that, in his distant home,
left the last dream like a burning fire,
he knows how to pray, good sister
you close the eyes of the children
at that hour when you close the roses.

L'ELEGIA DELLO SPERDUTO

O Nazareno, ti seguirò pregando
col Giordano accanto per compagno.

Il fiume dirà le laudi imparate lungo il suo cammino,
io risponderò, come baciando le parole
che sanno d'addii improvvisi
e di case abbandonate.

Sarò l'errante nella notte accesa,
con l'occhio impietrato a la più viva de le sette stelle,
l'amante sconosciuto dell'attesa
aggrappato al marmo de le sue mammelle.

THE ELEGY OF THE LOST

Nazarene, I will follow you in prayer
with the Jordan beside me as companion.

The river will sing the praises learned along its way,
I will answer, as if kissing words
that taste like sudden goodbyes
and deserted homes.

I will be the wanderer in the night,
my eyes turned to stones at the liveliest of seven stars,
the unknown lover of this waiting,
clasping its marble breasts.

IL FIORE DEL SILENZIO

Un cipressetto, un capitello di colonna dorica,
e il cielo fresco fresco del mattino
d'un mite colore di maiolica.

Dolore, o fonte eterna delle cose buone,
ecco il tuo tempio, la tua pietra sacra,
per il sonno che non ha tormento.

Non le piume odorose della alcove,
le rosse carezze d'una mano accesa,
intatto, ti daranno il fiore del silenzio.

THE FLOWER OF SILENCE

A little cypress, the capital of a Doric column,
and the freshest morning sky
was majolica.

Sorrow, the eternal font of good things,
here is your temple, your sacred stone,
for the sleep that knows no torment.

Not the scented feathers of alcoves,
but the red caresses of a burning hand,
will give you intact the flower of silence.

PROFANAZIONE

Ho ritrovato ancora più deserto
il mite giardino dei miei sogni.

Ditemi; ditemi chi colse i miei fiori
nati d'un tratto ne la sera
come un'idea non pensata mai!

Solo chi visse e non morì di sogni,
solo chi non sorrise innanzi al sole,
chi non sentì profumo di viole
colte in silenzio da mano di bambina,
solo chi non conobbe il pianto caldo
de l'anima malata, a stilla a stilla
colare nel dolore,
solo chi visse e non morì di sogni
lieve frusciò pel sacro mio giardino.

PROFANATION

I have found the mild garden of my dreams
all the more deserted.

Tell me; tell me who picked my flowers
born suddenly in the evening,
like an idea never thought?

Only who lived on and didn't die from dreams,
only who never smiled before the sun,
who didn't smell the scent of violets
picked in silence by the hand of a little girl,
only who didn't know the warm cry
of a sick soul, drop after drop,
dripping into sorrow,
only who lived on and didn't die from dreams,
but rustled lightly in my sacred garden.

ELIOSISMO

L'anima intatta, nel vaporoso grembiule di batista,
con gesto sacro, sparge la semente.

Bisogna amarla con occhio di purezza,
quando i suoi piedi nudi sfiorano la terra
e il sole le brucia la seta dei capelli:
ché la terra è il suo tempio,
e il sole suo Signore.

SOUL

The untouched soul, in the airy batiste apron,
with sacred gesture spreads seeds.

You have to love her with a pure eye,
when her naked feet skim the earth
and the sun burns the silk of her hair:
because the earth is her temple
and the sun is her Lord.

LA LUCE DEL SOLE

Bimbo, prega per l'alba e la notte,
fiore più azzurro del canto dell'usignolo
nel sogno degli amanti umili.

La notte ha le rose di tutte le leggende,
l'alba la porpora e il damasco delle reggie di gnomi,
le fontane che sbiancano come sciolte bende
e sanno, de le stelle, i tremuli nomi.

L'alba accende le fiaccole del sogno
nei silenzi delle pagode d'ametista;
piccolo agnello, il tuo lupo è il sole
che indora cimiteri dinanzi alla tua vista.

THE LIGHT OF THE SUN

Child, pray for the dawn and for the night,
a flower bluer than the song of the nightingale
in the dream of poor lovers.

The night has the roses of all legends,
the dawn has the purple and the damask of imagined palaces,
the fountains that blanch like loosened bandages
and know the trembling names of the stars.

Dawn lights the torches of dream
in the silences of amethyst pagodas;
little lamb, your wolf is the sun
that gilds graveyards before your eyes.

LA SERENITÀ

Non gettare il pane che t'avanza;
c'è qualcuno dietro la tua porta,
c'è chi non perde mai la speranza

se non vede la tua faccia torta.
E limpido, il chiaro del mattino
che, in silenzio, copre l'alba morta

dorme nei suoi occhi di bambino.

SERENITY

Don't throw away leftovers of bread;
there's someone behind your door,
there's someone whose hope's never lost

until they see your twisted face.
Serene, the morning light
silently covers the dead dawn

and sleeps in its childlike eyes.

LA PORTA CHIUSA

Viandante che trovasti chiusa
la porta della città straniera,
ch'era fiorita nella tua pupilla
come una serra di stelle,
torna a la piccola terra
tagliata dal mare, lontana;
ma tanto vicina al tuo cuore.

Chiudi nei sepolcri d'ombra della tua casa
i sogni delle azzurre lontananze;
ma, statuario, Re nel tuo rifugio,
scaccia dalla soglia immacolata
la porpora nova che veste l'antico cencioso
che barattò l'anima al primo crocicchio,
e, apri la porta, solo per tua madre.

THE LOCKED DOOR

Wanderer who found locked
the door of the foreign town,
that had flowered in your pupil
like a greenhouse of stars,
go back to the little land
cut by the sea, so far-off
and yet so close to your heart.

Lock in those shadows of home
the dreams of blue distances;
and, King of the Castle, drive away
from your immaculate threshold
the new purple robes of the old tramp
who rushed to sell his soul,
and only open the door to your mother.

NEI GIARDINI DELLA LUCE

Forse non sei nei giardini della luce
ove ti chiamano le fonti più accorate.

Nei sogni di camelia, apro le conchiglie
che mi dà il mare;
ne l'incanto stellare,
pescatore di perle, non trovo che fanghiglie.

Cerco, a sera, la lucciola più viva,
quella che fa lume, nei boschi di narcisi,
a la formica tardiva;
ma vedo, solo, tremiti divisi
di smorti chiarori, su la brina.

Forse non sei nei giardini della luce.

IN THE GARDENS OF LIGHT

Perhaps you aren't in the gardens of light
where the tormented springs are calling you.

In the dreams of camellia,
I open the shells that the sea gives me;
in the enchantment of the stars,
pearl-fisher, all I find is slime.

In the evening I look for the liveliest glow-worm
that sheds light in the woods of narcissi
to the tardy ant;
yet I only see, on the hoarfrost,
the split slivers of a dull dim light.

Perhaps you aren't in the gardens of light.

NUVOLETTE NEL VESPERO

O bianchi cavallini di felicità
che le stellucce d'oro avete per sonagli:
fermatevi un poco ne la mia città.

C'è l'acqua più fresca per la vostra sete,
il fieno più buono per la vostra fame.

Noi amiamo i casolari di pietrisco,
dove le mani dure, in ciotole d'argilla,
ci danno da bere come ai bimbi.

Le vostre fonti di marmo sono avvelenate,
il vostro fieno è amaro, come il pane
che date in elemosina.

LITTLE EVENING CLOUDS

Little happy horses
with little golden stars for bells:
stop for a little while in my hometown.

We have the freshest water if you are thirsty,
We have the best hay if you are hungry.

We love stony farmhouses,
where hard hands, in clay bowls,
give us drink like children.

Your marble springs are poisoned,
and your hay bitter, just like the bread
you give as alms to the needy.

LA RONDINE DI LUCE

L'amore è una rondine di luce
che vola dal mio al tuo giardino
e ricama parole di cristallo
ne la notte che s'apre come una nuvola di mirra.

Sei forse l'armonia, chiusa
come una violetta nel mio cuore
che cerca nel cielo, povera delusa,
il primo raggio, il primo luccicore?

Al mattino la rondine beve ad una fonte
dove l'acqua è un cespo di farfalle
che parlano di fiori
accanto a tre piccoli cipressi,
tre piccoli sogni addormentati.

Tu prega che la fonte non si dissecchi mai;
a mani giunte, starò ad ascoltare
la musica d'oro frusciare su l'arpa del crepuscolo,
o fascio di glicinie socchiuse come le palpebre
ne la malinconia di chi disse: addio!

THE SWALLOW OF LIGHT

Love is a swallow of light
that flies from my garden to yours
and embroiders crystal words
in the night that unfolds like a cloud of myrrh.

Are you harmony, perhaps, locked
in my heart like a violet
that, disillusioned, looks in the sky
for the first ray, the first sparkle?

In the morning the swallow drinks at a well
where water is a spray of butterflies
that talk about flowers
near three little cypresses,
three small sleeping dreams.

Pray that the well will never dry;
with joined hands, I will listen
to the golden music rustle on the sunset's harp,
a sheaf of wisteria, half-closed like eyelids
in the melancholy of one who said: "Goodbye"!

LA MUSICA DEGLI ANGIOLI

Poliziano, amico dolce d'altri tempi,
non verranno nei giardini, come nella tua ballata,
a cogliere le rose le fanciulle,
e non sarà la principessa della fiaba
– fiorellino d'oro piegato tra le foglie di tulle –
a darmi il bacio sopra gli occhi stanchi,
quando la sera porta via la luce.

Jacopone, forse ne l'ora prima
che s'alza dal mare come un petalo di rosa
udii le tue laudi d'intorno,
come bisbigli d'uccelli purissimi
che volino incontro al sole,
e mi parve d'esserti vicino
a baciarti e a piangere,
mentre le labbra staccavano dall'anima
le parole più buone, per offrirtele come fiori di campo.

THE MUSIC OF ANGELS

Poliziano, dear old friend,
young ladies won't go to the gardens
to pick flowers, like in your ballad,
and it won't be the fabled princess
– golden flower folded among leaves of tulle –
who will kiss my tired eyes
when the evening light is gone.

Jacopone, perhaps in the first hour
that rises from the sea like the petal of a rose,
I heard your prayers all around me,
like the whispers of the purest birds
flying towards the sun,
and it felt as if I were close to you
to kiss you and cry,
as my lips took the sweet words from the soul
and offered them up to you like wild flowers.

ORO SU LA NEVE

Ti aveva cercato, la mia anima di puro orientale,
fra gli usignoli nei cirri turchini delle foreste,
quando il cielo aveva scaglie di colori come l'opale,
quando la notte era un mosaico celeste.

Ti trovo ne la luce, come in una reggia,
presso lo zampillo d'una fonte che, come un piumino
incipria l'azzurro. Sei forse la stella che galleggia
sul lago de la sera e affonda nel mattino

per trovarsi, goccia di rugiada,
su le labbra socchiuse d'una mammola.

Il tuo nome lo ricama il sole,
con oro sottile su la neve;
preghiera d'una sillaba un angiolo lo legge
e l'insegna agli uccelli con la musica lieve
d'un arco di seta sui raggi della luce.

E gli uccelli lo trillano a le rose,
e le rose, col tuo nome, si profumano.

GOLD ON SNOW

My pure oriental soul had looked for you,
among nightingales in the deep blue cirrus of the woods,
when the sky had shades of colour like opal,
when the night was a blue mosaic.

I find you in the light, as in a palace,
near the up-welling of a spring which, like a piece of down,
powders the blue. Perhaps you are the star that floats
on the lake of the night and sinks in the morning

to find itself, a dew drop,
on the half-closed lips of a violet.

The sun embroiders your name,
with thin gold, on the snow;
a simple prayer, an angel reads it
and teaches it to the birds with the faint music
of a silk bow on the rays of light.

And the birds sing it to the roses,
and the roses are scented with your name.

LA FONTANA NOTTURNA

Profumo di zagara chiusa, fontana notturna d'incanti,
io ti chiamo coi nomi dei fiori più fragili,
quando il sonno mi manca,
– il mio pane con la croce bianca,
tutta di stelle e neve –.

Quando, vispa, sui muri degli orti,
saltella
la lupinella,
io cerco tra il roseo i tuoi occhi
così calmi che sembrano d'una pecorella;

ma che mi fanno tanto male:
come le parole d'addio,
come le parole non dette
che restano nel cuore
per tema di trovarle poco affettuose.

Lasciai due baci sul tuo corpo d'orchidea,
che a me parvero due margheritine,
di quelle che stanno sui lembi delle strade
e sono piccole piccole ed hanno tanto freddo,
e, fuori, il cielo a macchie scure e bianche come una pernice
aveva la mia febbre, e io credevo d'essere felice.

THE NIGHT FOUNTAIN

The scent of an orange blossom, an enchanted night fountain,
I call you with the names of the most delicate flowers
when sleep escapes me,
– my bread with the white cross,
all stars and snow – .

When lively on the garden walls
the violet
dances,
I look among the purple for your eyes
so calm like those of a lamb;

and yet they hurt me so much:
like words of farewell,
like words that remain
unspoken in the heart
for fear of finding them too cold.

I left two kisses on your orchid body,
they looked like two little daisies,
like those which grow at the roadside,
so small and suffering the cold,
and the sky, dappled like a bird,
bore my fever, and I thought I was happy.

I SEMI DELLA LUCE

Certo, odorano i cedri bagnati di rugiada,
ma io sento, solo, la tua bocca: stella di profumo;
certo, l'alba sparge i semi della luce,
ma io vedo perché mi guardano i tuoi occhi.

Ti scolpirò sul petalo d'una magnolia,
nei boschi di mirra, ove i notturni dei zampilli,
ne le culle di raso, addormentano farfalle.

THE SEEDS OF LIGHT

Sure, the fragrant cedars are wet with dew
but I smell your mouth only: scented star;
sure, the dawn spreads the seeds of light,
but I see because your eyes look at me.

I will sketch you in the petal of a magnolia,
in woods of myrrh, where at night sounds of water
soothe butterflies to sleep in satin cradles.

LA PUREZZA

Quale sarà domani il mio poema,
o donna nata dal mio sogno mistico!
Ti fermerò nel più soave distico,
marmo intatto con mano che non trema.

La mia pupilla che vegliò estatica
il cielo della notte orientale
per luce avrà la stella più serafica,
per non toccarti con febbre sensuale.

PURITY

What will my poem be tomorrow,
woman born from my mystic dream!
I will keep you in the sweetest couplet,
untouched marble with steady hand.

My eye that watched in ecstasy
over the sky of an eastern night
will have the most seraphic star for light,
not to touch you with its sensual fire.

MENTRE BRUCIA LA MIRRA

Ma canteremo, canteremo invano
tutte le rose delle nostre serre,
gli acri profumi di spumose terre,
laghi di sogni del color del ciano;

l'albe civette sorte da un lavacro
di fiordalisi azzurri e di viole
subitamente smorte innanzi al sole
grande e sereno come un fuoco sacro?

Ma sul capo ci volano le stelle,
come farfalle che con lenti frulli
d'ali biancastre su per campi brulli
vanno ne l'ombra in cerca di fiammelle.

THE BURNING MYRRH

So will we sing, will we sing in vain
all the roses in our greenhouses,
the bitter perfume of rich lands,
lakes of sky-blue dreams;

white owls risen from a bath
of blue cornflowers and violets
withered at once before the sun,
big and serene like a sacred fire?

Stars fly over our heads,
like butterflies that with the slow whirr
of white wings over barren fields
go into the dark looking for flames.

NOTES

p. 21 The epigraph from *Macbeth* (Act 4, Scene III, line 242) was used by Quasimodo to open his Nobel Lecture – *Il poeta e il politico* (The poet and the politician) – delivered in Stockholm on 11 November 1959 (www.nobel.se/laureates/literature-1959-lecture.html). Quasimodo was awarded The Nobel Prize for Literature "for his lyrical poetry, which with classical fire expresses the tragic experience of life in our own times".

p. 61 In 'Music of Angels', Jacopone (Todi, c. 1230-1236; Collazzone, 1306) and Poliziano (Montepulciano, 1454; Firenze 1494), are among the founding fathers and undisputed masters of the Italian poetic tradition.

p. 71 In 'The Burning Myrrh', "ciano" is a literary term and can mean cerulean or pale blue; in the context of this poem, sky-blue seemed an appropriate choice.

GLENDALOUGH

During his visit to Ireland in February 1963, Quasimodo went to Glendalough, one of the country's oldest sites. He later recalled this visit in an eponymous poem, which it seemed appropriate to include in this volume. Despite the translators' best efforts, Quasimodo's 'Glendalough' defied translation. Their response is in the two new Glendalough poems, one in verse and one in prose.

SALVATORE QUASIMODO

GLENDALOUGH

I morti di Glendalough
sottò le croci celtiche guardano da un monte
fluido di nubi nere
e corte. Dicono che fuggono la primavera,
ascoltano lentamente i rovesci
di pioggia e le ombre dei corvi
che passano e seguono lassù parole
bianche di ponente. Sono amici
questi morti dei burroni,
compagni del mare che più in là
si curva di bufere e incastra
le onde con la luna. I nomi dei celti
sono d'allarme e di rombi illusi.
Vicino a un torrente, sotto il sole,
non c'era né tempesta né il romantico
crepuscolo di mezzogiorno,
e solo un corvo ghignava
dal cielo, ricordando una Donna bellissima
morta d'amore dentro il convento di Kevin
dal tetto a imbuto.

1964

GERALD DAWE

GLENDALOUGH
after Salvatore Quasimodo

Under Celtic crosses the dead
of Glendalough look out
from a mountain of clouds.
They evade Spring, listening
to the downpour and the crows
that fly with westerly words.

The dead are friends of the gorges,
companions of the sea
that a little further on bends
with storms and traps the waves
alongside the moon. Names speak
of alarm, disenchanted thunder.

Near a stream, under the sun,
neither storm nor midday sunset.
Only the one crow in the sky
calling about a woman
who died of love inside the funnel-
shaped roof of Kevin's hideaway.

2001

Marco Sonzogni

GLENDALOUGH
after Salvatore Quasimodo

alone and mirrored clear in love's deep river
    – Seamus Heaney, 'St. Kevin and the blackbird'

Le mie croci e i miei morti li enumero ovunque: e da questa valle di burroni e corsi d'acqua, e da questo sito di pietre e di pensieri, e da questa cella, di Caoimhín – amico di preti e di poeti, di misteri e di merli – mi ritornano a parlare, voce millenaria, tramite te: e i due laghi si tingono del colore dei tuoi occhi – verde bagnato, verde pagano – di donna taumaturga, messaggera celtica, ultimo grembo di verità e di amore. Qui ora sei compagna del santo cristiano per mitigare il dolore del distacco e della lontananza, per riparare ai torti di chi tortura e di chi distrugge l'anima del mondo. E mentre il sole abdica alla luna in questa sera d'inizio primavera – fertile vigilia, consumato viatico – tu mi lasci nella speranza della preghiera e sulle ali di un corvo ritorni nella pace del silenzio.

2005

BIOGRAPHICAL NOTES

SALVATORE QUASIMODO was born of Sicilian parents in Modica, near Syracuse, in 1901. Interested in becoming an engineer, he enrolled at the Politecnico in Rome, also studying Latin and Greek at the University there, but did not complete his studies. He obtained a position with the Italian government's civil engineering corps, and in 1930 saw the publication of three poems in the avant-garde magazine *Solaria*, and then his first full-length collection, *Acque e terre* (Waters and Lands). Two years later, his second collection, *Oboe sommerso* (Sunken Oboe) appeared.

In 1938, he left his government position and became editor of the weekly magazine, *Tempo*; three years later he was appointed to the Chair of Italian Literature at the Giuseppe Verdi Conservatory in Milan.

An outspoken anti-Fascist during the Second World War, and for a while a member of the Communist Party, he published three collections during the 1940s: *Nuove Poesie* (New Poems), 1942; *Giorno dopogiorno* (Day after Day), 1946, and *La vita non è sogno* (Life Is Not a Dream), 1949. He also became known as a translator – of the Greek and Roman lyric and epic poets (Sophocles, Aeschylus, Euripides, Ovid and Virgil among them), Shakespeare, Molière and twentieth-century writers such as Neruda and e.e. cummings.

Quasimodo was awarded the Etna-Taormina International Prize in Poetry along with Dylan Thomas in 1953 and, in 1959, the Nobel Prize for literature – "for his lyrical poetry, which with classical fire expresses the tragic experience of life in our own times". His last book of verse was *Dare e avere* (To Give and To Have), 1966.

Quasimodo died in Naples on 14 June 1968.

GERALD DAWE was born in Belfast, Northern Ireland, in 1952. His first book of poems, *Sheltering Places*, was published in 1978. It was followed by *The Lundys Letter, Sunday School, Heart of Hearts, The Morning Train, Lake Geneva* and *Points West*. He has also published *The Proper Word: Collected Criticism*, and *My Mother City*, as well as editing various anthologies of Irish poetry and criticism. Dawe has taught at NUI, Galway, Thomond College, University of Limerick and at Boston College where he was the Burns Visiting Professor. He is a fellow of Trinity College Dublin. A recipient of the Macaulay Fellowship in Literature, a Ledig-Rowohlt Fondation Award, a

Hawthornden International Writers' Fellowship and literature awards from the Arts Council of Ireland, he has given readings and lectures in many parts of the world. He lives in County Dublin, Ireland.

Marco Sonzogni was born in Mortara (Italy) in 1971. He holds degrees from the University of Pavia, Almo Collegio Borromeo; the National University of Ireland, Dublin; the University of Dublin, Trinity College; and Victoria University of Wellington, New Zealand, where he is a Lecturer in the School of Languages and Cultures (Italian Programme) and a member of the New Zealand Centre for Literary Translation. He is a widely published critic, editor, reviewer and literary translator. His first collection of poems and translations, *Assenze*, was published in 2005; his second book, *Chiaroscuro*, will appear in 2009. A recipient of research grants and awards, he is currently working on James Joyce, Katherine Mansfield, Alda Merini and Eugenio Montale. He lives in Wellington, New Zealand.

Also available in the Arc Publications'
ARCANIA: NEW TRANSLATIONS OF CLASSIC POETS

ROSE AUSLÄNDER
Mother Tongue: Selected Poems
Translated from the German by
Jean Boase-Beier and Anthony Vivis

FRANCO FORTINI
Poems
Translated from the Italian by
Michael Hamburger

GEORG TRAKL
To the Silenced: Selected Poems
Translated from the German and introduced by
Will Stone

ED. PETER ORAM
The Page and The Fire
POEMS BY RUSSIAN POETS ON RUSSIAN POETS
Selected, translated from the Russian and introduced by
Peter Oram